praise for paul ferrini's books

"These words embody tolerance, universality, love and compassion – hallmarks of all Great Teachings. They turn our attention inward to our own divine nature, instead of diverting it outward. Paul Ferrini is a modern-day Kahlil Gibran—poet, mystic, visionary, teller of truth." Larry Dossey, M.D., author of *Healing Words: The Power of Prayer and the Practice of Medicine.*

"Paul Ferrini leads us skillfully and courageously beyond shame, blame and attachment to our wounds into the depths of self-forgiveness. His work is a must-read for all people who are ready to take responsibility for their own healing." John Bradshaw, author of *Family Secrets.*

"A breath of fresh air in an often musty and cluttered domain. With sweetness, clarity, and simplicity we are directed to the truth within. I read this book whenever my heart directs, which is often." Pat Rodegast, author of *Emmanuel's Book I, II and III.*

"Paul Ferrini's writing is authentic, delightful and wise. It reconnects the reader to the Spirit Within, to that place where even our deepest wounds can be healed." Joan Borysenko, Ph.D., author of *Guilt is the Teacher, Love is the Answer.*

"I feel that this work comes from a continuous friendship with the deepest part of the Self. I trust its wisdom." Coleman Barks, poet and translator.

"Paul Ferrini's wonderful books show a way to walk lightly with joy on planet earth." Gerald Jampolsky, M.D., author of *Love is Letting Go of Fear.*

"Paul Ferrini leads us on a gentle i̶ ̶ ̶ ̶ ̶ ̶ joy and happiness – inside oursel ̶ ̶ ̶ *The Handbook of Higher Consciou.*

Book Design by Paul Ferrini
Typesetting by Nancy Jean Barmashi
Artwork by Lucy Mueller White

For Elisabeth Kubler-Ross
and Stephen Camp

ISBN # 1-879159-18-1

Manufactured in the United States of America

the
ecstatic
moment

a practical manual
for opening your heart
and staying in it

paul ferrini

table of contents

one ◆ the ecstatic moment

two ◆ practice

three ◆ learning to listen

four ◆ an angel's song of waking

part one

the ecstatic

moment

In the ecstatic moment

you recognize your spiritual perfection and that of all other beings. Perfection is never about the past or the future. It is always and only about now. You are perfect right now, regardless of what you are thinking or feeling, regardless of all your perceived problems or unfinished business.

You are acceptable as you are, no matter how many mistakes you think you have made. There is nothing you have thought, felt, or done that prevents you from realizing your perfection right here and right now.

All suffering results from your refusal to accept and bless your life just the way it is now, from your insecure need to try to fix yourself, your relationships and the world you live in. When you stop finding fault with your life and trying to fix it, you can be in it more fully. When you are in your life fully, it has energy, purpose and integrity. There is nothing lacking, nothing insufficient, nothing broken. It is perfect just as it is.

In the ecstatic moment

you also recognize that others are perfect just the way they are. They are perfect regardless of how they have behaved toward you in the past or how you think they might behave toward you in the future. They are perfect regardless of how many problems they appear to have. They do not need to be redeemed, improved or fixed. They are entitled to their experience, whether or not they like it, you like it, or anyone else likes it or agrees with it.

Each person is whole and complete even though he may not believe it himself, even though others may see him as deficient. If you would see a person through the eyes of Spirit you will look past his apparent weaknesses and see his inner perfection. Even if he attacks you, you will see that he just wants your love and doesn't know how to ask for it.

When you have judgments about others, it is helpful to be aware of those judgments. Don't seek to justify them. Don't beat yourself for having them. Just realize that you cannot see whom anyone is when you are judging that person.

What you judge in another shows you some aspect of yourself you haven't yet come to accept. When you learn to love and accept this part of yourself, you won't need to make judgments about others.

In the ecstatic moment

you also recognize that the outside world is acceptable just the way it is. It doesn't need to be changed or fixed or improved. It doesn't have to meet your expectations.

Suffering arises when you want things to be different than they are. Things can never be different than they are. What can be different is the meaning you give to what happens. You can't change what happens, but you can change what you think it means.

What you don't like in the world reflects what you haven't come to embrace in yourself. As you learn to love yourself more completely, fewer outside situations will disturb you.

Suffering also arises when you become attached to certain circumstances of your life or roles that you play. All roles and circumstances eventually become limiting; if you are to grow, these must change. Although you are not always ready for it, change is liberating. It calls you to a deeper level of Self. By constantly shedding your external identifications, you give birth to that which cannot be defined from without, that which is everpresent and eternal within you.

perception is the key

When you realize the perfection of everything as it is, you see that every outcome is a good one. The world will never be good unless you are willing to see its goodness. What you experience depends on how you look at things. When you look with judgment, life is twisted and empty. When you look with an open heart and mind, life is poignant and full of meaning.

Whatever you see without love and acceptance, you separate from. You do this because you are afraid. Separation may seem to deaden your fear for a while, but in the end it only adds to it, deepening your sense of disconnection and victimhood.

Like all defense mechanisms born of fear, separation is an illusion. As soon as you look again with love, you see a different world.

what you are responsible for

You are responsible for your thoughts, feelings and experience. You are not responsible for the thoughts, feelings and experiences of others. It is not your responsibility that someone else is happy or sad.

However, you are responsible for being happy or sad, fulfilled or unfulfilled. Your joy and your anger are your responsibility. You cannot make anyone else responsible for how you think or feel. The attempt to do so just slows down your awakening process.

You are here to love and accept yourself, to embrace and learn from your experience. You are not here to take care of anyone else or to be taken care of by anyone else.

You are here to be who you are authentically. You are not here to please others or to win their approval. Even though you risk losing someone's approval, you are responsible for telling that person the truth of your experience.

You are here to make your own decisions and to learn from your own mistakes. You are not here to make decisions for other people, nor to let others make decisions for you.

You are here to learn to love and take care of yourself, to nurture yourself, to be in touch with your feelings, to express yourself in a creative way. You are here to honor yourself in all ways, to know what feels good for you and to do it, and to know what does not feel good to you and to refrain from doing it or allowing it to be done to you.

You are responsible for whatever is happening right now. You are responsible for everything you ask for and for everything you agree to do. You are not a victim of anyone else's actions.

Victims need to please others to gain approval. They say *yes* when they mean *no*. Then they resent the other person for "coercing" them. In truth, they betray themselves by not saying *no* to things they don't want to do.

Your responsibility is to say *yes* when you mean *yes* and to say *no* when you mean *no*. Do not say *yes* when you mean *no*. If you do, whatever happens will be your responsibility.

If you change your mind about an agreement, tell the other person right away. As soon as you know what you want, communicate it to the others involved. Making a mistake is not a problem if you take responsibility for it and act swiftly to correct it.

Don't try to make others responsible for the choices you make. That is emotional cowardice. Take responsibility for your choices and for the mistakes you will inevitably make. Acknowledge your transgressions and learn from them so that you do not repeat them.

If you treat another in an unfair way, tell him that you realize that you acted unfairly and that you are learning to act with greater integrity and compassion. Ask for his understanding and for-giveness. Few beings will withhold forgiveness when they see that you feel remorse for your transgressions and are taking steps to correct them. In the same manner, do not withhold from others the understanding and forgiveness they request from you.

What happens is perfect, but that includes all the mistakes that you make. To be perfect does not mean to be mistake free. It's okay to fail. It's okay to learn from your mistakes.

Whatever happens is okay. Everything is important. Everything is forgivable.

what you're not responsible for

You are not responsible for the thoughts, feelings or experience of other people, even if you are involved in their lives. Others are respon-sible for every thought or feeling they have. When they try to blame you or make you responsible for what has happened to them, they are not acting in good faith. Do not take false responsibility for the thoughts, feelings and experience of others. It does not help them or you.

Your responsibility is to accept and honor what others are experiencing, but not to take responsibility for it. Their experience belongs to them alone.

In order to accept and honor the experience of others, you must refrain from judging it, interpreting it, analyzing it, comparing it to your experience. You may ask open-ended questions to help people communicate their experience fully, but these questions must not have their own agenda. Their entire purpose must be to enable others to communicate what they are attempting to convey to you.

Your responsibility is to listen deeply and fully to the communication of others. It is not to agree or disagree with what they have to say. Your agreement or disagreement is irrelevant at best, and intrusive at worst.

You are here to create a safe, open, loving space for yourself and other people. You do this by staying in your own life and out of the lives of other people. You do this by taking responsibility for your thoughts, feelings and experiences, and inviting others to do the same. You do it by honoring what works for you, by being clear about it and committed to it, and by honoring what works for others by encouraging them to be clear about it and committed to it.

These boundary lines are self-explanatory. However, they are profoundly difficult to adhere to on an ongoing basis. Most people have learned patterns of codependence, mutual trespass and betrayal. Reversing this conditioning is a challenging proposition. It requires ongoing practice with a partner and/or with a group of people. Dedicated practice adhering to these boundaries in human relationships will result in a life that is more centered and peaceful, as well as more compassionate and connected to others.

To summarize then: accept and be responsible for your own experience. Accept the experience of others, but do not take responsibility for it. Do not make decisions for others or let others make decisions for you. Do not be an authority for anyone else or let anyone else be an authority for you. Understand that you know what is best for you and others know what is best for them. This is true even though you and others make mistakes. Those mistakes are part of the spiritual perfection of life. Give yourself the freedom to make mistakes and learn from them. Give others the same freedom.

Don't make others responsible for your thoughts, feelings or experience. What you think, feel and experience belongs only to you. When you project this responsibility onto others, become aware of it and with humility take it back.

Don't allow others to make you responsible for their thoughts, feelings or experience. What they think, feel and experience belongs only to them. When others project this responsibility onto you, tell them in a non-blaming, compassionate way that you cannot accept this responsibility and would like to support them in taking responsibility for their own experience.

To put it simply: be who you are. Encourage others to be who they are. Be authentic, responsible, and empowered. Empower others to be authentic and responsible.

Don't lead. Don't follow. Go alone when you have to. Go hand in hand when others want to join you. Either way, be an equal. See your inherent equality with all beings. That way your gifts will be offered in a way that helps others and you will receive the gifts of others in a way that helps you.

the horn of plenty

When Jesus had many people to feed, he used what was present and found that there were many loaves and fishes to go around. When you accept the present moment as it is, it is always enough. Most of your argument with life comes from your belief that there is not enough to go around. If your wife falls in love with another man, you think you are losing love. If someone takes your money, you think you will never have any.

These fear-based thoughts are not true. You think them because you would rather pity yourself than empower yourself. You would rather pretend to be a victim than take responsibility.

It is just as easy to think in an empowering way. If you have loved one person, you know that you are capable of love, so you know absolutely that you will create more love in your life. If you have made money, then you know you are capable of making more.

Whatever comes from you cannot be taken away. Not your love. Not your money. Not your time. Not your life.

Only what comes from others can be given and taken away. But your gift cannot be taken away from you. Whenever you give it, you increase your confidence in the gift and your ability to give it.

There is always more of a good thing. If love feels good to you, there will be more of it. If money feels good to you, you will attract more of it. If what you do with your time feels good, you will have more time to do it.

But if you do not enjoy your love or your money or your time, you will have less of it. What you do not enjoy does not prosper. What you do out of sacrifice or guilt becomes problematic and difficult. It shrinks when you wish it would expand.

If you have four fishes and you don't enjoy them, don't be surprised if you have only two fishes five minutes from now. In ten minutes, don't be surprised if you start running around saying "Where have all the fishes gone?" or "why me, God?"

The universe does not support what you do out of sacrifice or guilt. It's that simple.

You can do a million affirmations and it won't make any difference. If you are acting out of sacrifice or guilt, you will not experience abundance. If your work and responsibility grow, so will the hardship attached to them.

Many people want to be helpers, but they do not help themselves. They feed others, but they do not feed themselves. Is it any wonder that they burn out, become tired and disillusioned?

If you are not fed by what you do, how can you feed others? If your job does not feed you, how can you give your gift to it? If your relationship does not feed you, how you can celebrate your beloved? If your lifestyle does not feed you, how can you experience joy in your life?

Your happiness is not secondary. It is of primary importance. Abundance flows from your happiness. The gifts of God flow through your love and acceptance of yourself.

A world based on sacrifice is not a happy or abundant world. It is a world in which there never seems to be enough and we are always looking around to see if someone has more than we do.

It is a world in which love, and therefore resources, seem to be in limited supply. But since resources flow from love and acceptance, the transformation of scarcity in our lives always begins in our own consciousness.

The question "Am I loving myself and caring for my own life?" must be asked. "Am I doing work that I enjoy doing, work that enables me to express my gift? Am I in a relationship in which I am able to give and receive love? Is my partner a true equal? Do we honor each other and make decisions together?" All these questions must be asked if we want to understand the issues of scarcity and abundance.

When you are honest, you see that the aspects of your life that prosper are the ones that you enjoy the most and the ones to which you give your greatest energy and commitment. What you don't enjoy or give your full attention and commitment to does not prosper.

Whispering a few magical words will not change the emotional allegiance we are referring to. It takes an inner revolution, in which the feet and the hands learn to listen to and align with the heart. What we "do" must be consistent with who we "are." That is the formula for the flow of love and abundance in our lives.

The truth is there is always enough. But we are asking the wrong question. We are asking "what needs to be done and how can I do it?"

24

when the real question is "who am I and how can I give my gift?"

Until I know who I am and what my gift is, anything I do will be done out of insecurity. I will focus on helping you express your gift. I will try to live my life through your vision and your work. I will work for you instead of for myself.

But when I ask the questions "Who am I?" and "What is my gift and how can I express it?" I come to the beginning, the alpha point, in my journey to authenticity. And that is a profound, baptismal moment. I anoint and empower myself. I accept and commit to my calling.

Each one must do this, or individuation cannot happen. The child must cut the umbilical cord. He must bow to the parents and step into his own life. He must give up the security of his parent's home to test his own wings.

A child who stays in his parent's house never grows to maturity. A student who remains with his teacher once he has learned his craft does not become an artist in his own right. A human being who allows himself to be defined by the expectations of society and the significant others in his life, never gives himself permission to discover who he is, what his gift is, and how he can give it.

How can he reach into the horn of plenty as Jesus did and pull out all the resources that are needed if he does not know who he is or what he has to give? Of course, he cannot! A man must go within himself, discover the grail, and carry it through the inner darkness if he is to emerge empowered from the cave of self.

To ask "What needs to be done here?" is the wrong question. Because when you ask it, some-one always answers it in a way that does not empower you. "Oh, so glad you asked. The floor needs to be swept, the dishes need to be done, and the trash needs to be taken out....and, oh yes, if you have time........" There's always work to be done when someone else is setting the agenda.

How many people answer the question "What needs to be done?" accurately. How many people say "why, nothing needs to be done here." How many people ask "what would you like to do?"

If you do not learn to feed yourself, who will feed you? If you do not discover your gift and give it wholeheartedly, who will give their gift to you?

When one person has a fish and gives it, and another has some bread and offers it, a feast is born. There is always enough when you are giving your gift and others are giving theirs. There is never enough when nobody knows what gift to bring.

Every moment is abundant, whole and complete. There is enough in this moment to feed you and everybody else. But don't ask "what needs to be done?" Instead, ask "What gift can I offer now?"

When your gift has been offered with no strings attached, it multiplies. One fish becomes two. And two become four. Your gift feeds others. And they feed their friends in turn. In this manner the multitude is fed.

When we think of the loaves and the fishes, we often see it as a solo job. But Jesus was showing all of us what we too would one day do. He was inviting us to the harvest of an empowered community, where every person's gift is authentic and an essential part of the meal of life.

if I am not for myself

When we act because we are joyful, our actions uplift others. Giving our gift inspires others. This simple existential act is essentially generous.

Rabbi Hillel said: " If I am not for myself, who is for me? But if I am for myself alone, who am I? If not now, when?"

"If I am not for myself, who is for me?" One who does not discover the gift and learn to give it does not feel loved and supported. No matter how many opportunities for self-expression present themselves in his life, he cannot take advantage of them. Not knowing what his gift is, he does not recognize the opportunities for giving that come his way. Not knowing who he is, he cannot let others know him. He remains an untapped potential, an enigmatic face that says to others "Please don't look here; I'm not ready to be seen."

But one who knows himself and his gift lets the world know who he is. He shares himself. He gives joyfully of himself. People notice and appreciate him for his commitment and sincerity. He inspires others. His gift is not just for himself. That is just the beginning of it.

"If I am for myself alone, who am I?" If I act only for my own benefit my gift doesn't help anybody. People look at me with envy. They resent my success. They don't feel empowered around me. When I act for myself alone, I don't make many friends. I don't experience the gratitude and appreciation of the people whose lives I touch. The energy I put out does not return to me. I get tired. I don't feel appreciated. I'm not sure I want to give my gift anymore.

It is impossible for me to be for myself alone and continue to give the gift. When I am for myself alone, the circle of giving and receiving is broken. The energy I put out does not return to me, so I do not have sufficient energy to continue giving.

"If not now, when?" If I am not giving my gift now, when will I give it? If I am not giving my gift without strings attached, when will I do so? If I am not empowering others through my self expression, when will I start? Hillel reminds us that "not now" means "not ever." For now is the only time there is.

If you are not joyfully expressing yourself in this moment, when do you propose to do it? Tomorrow? Next week?

Perhaps you feel you have to go back to school and get another degree to give yourself permission to be joyful right now. Or maybe there is some other condition you place on the expression of your joy. That, of course, is your choice. But there are no prerequisites to the expression of your joy in this moment. Whatever requisites you see are the ones you made up.

For the ego, there are hundreds if not thousands of hoops to jump through before we have its permission to be joyful or worthy of love. But every one of these hoops is self-created and superfluous. We can throw them all away and be joyful and worthy of love right now.

If I am not for myself, how can you be for me? If I do not love myself, how can I receive your love? It is not possible. I must find a way to love and accept myself and then I will be able to benefit from your love and support.

Once I love myself and express myself creatively, I can extend my love and self-conviction enthusiastically to you. I can remind you that you too can do as I have done. I can become a model to you of what is possible. That is what Jesus did. He became a role model for us. He told us that we could do as he did.

And so my empowerment becomes your empowerment and yours becomes another's. From a single light, all lamps may be lit. But there is more than a single lamp burning. There are hundreds of thousands of lamps burning on the planet. The way is well-lit for those who are seeking it.

If you are not joyful now, when will you be joyful? Ask yourself, "If not now, when?" And then be the joy you wish you were feeling. Be the love you want. Be the gift.

That is joy's way.

In this moment, everything is present. All gifts can be discovered and given. Nothing that is needed is lacking.

If we perceive something as lacking, it can mean only one thing: our gift has not yet been given. How can heaven be here right now if we are withholding our love? Heaven happens only when we are giving all of our love in this moment.

beauty's way

Beauty's way is simple and elegant. Everything happens in its own time and place.

The river may overflow its banks or it may shrink to a trickle. Seasons of drought and high water are inevitable. But sooner or later, the river will reach the sea. The outcome is certain. No matter how far we stray from our essential nature, we will return to it. Our destiny is to become who we already are.

Our moments of greatest ecstasy and peace are found when we accept ourselves just as we are. In that acceptance, we demonstrate our trust in the river. When we trust the river, it carries us where we need to go.

The river knows what we need better than we do. We are too short sighted and opinionated to know what will serve us best. Yet we think we know. We paint pictures in our minds of how things should be. We establish conditions for our own happiness.

Whenever we do that, the river takes us for an unexpected ride. And, moan and groan as we may, there is nothing that we can do about it. If we don't surrender to the river now, we will surrender later.

Our surrender is inevitable. When we oppose the river and try to swim upstream, we find out that the river is larger and stronger than we are. If we struggle, we will unnecessarily tire and wound ourselves.

If we dive in, embrace our life as it is, and let the river take us downstream, we will come to the next step in our lives. In truth it is not a step. It is an allowing. It happens through us and with us. We do not make it happen.

Surrender cannot happen without acceptance. If cannot happen without trust. Forget all the other prerequisites. They aren't about surrender.

Surrender happens right now, not in the future. Surrender happens when you accept your life as it is and trust where it is leading you.

Surrender leads to bliss. It leads to ecstasy. It leads to the recognition of the essential rightness of every aspect of your life, even the ones that sometimes make you uncomfortable.

If you are not feeling ecstasy, you are not accepting your life as it is. You are not trusting the river.

Resistance results in chronic fault-finding and unhappiness. Trying to change yourself or your partner only reinforces the belief that you or your partner are not okay. Trying to fix some perception of lack in your life only reinforces that perception. It has nothing to do with reality.

In reality, you lack nothing. In reality, there is nothing to fix, because nothing is wrong.

The perception and subsequent belief that

there is something wrong creates feelings of scarcity, victimhood, and inadequacy. These feelings are real only in as much as they reflect your state of consciousness. However, that state of consciousness is temporary and insubstantial. When you stop finding fault, these feelings disappear.

The question is, "what remains when the perception of lack disappears?" What remains is the inherent rightness, the natural abundance of all things. What remains is the river flowing simply, elegantly, toward the sea.

Beneath the apparent complexity, the constant vying of egos for control and attention, there is a simple rhythm that enables each one of us to individuate. The river carries each of us forward. It helps us honor ourselves and become who we are.

As we grow confident in being and expressing ourselves, we are naturally carried into a greater whole. Two small rivers merge into a mighty river or empty into a shining lake. No longer separate, they become one presence, one consciousness. They have a new purpose, a new trust, which they can honor only by coming together. At last, the beloved has arrived.

In the end, all the rivers and lakes empty into the ocean, in which the planet swims and has its being. All forms of love merge into divine, unconditional love, the essence of who and what we are.

All of us are pulled by an inner current to be born, to grow, to individuate, and to merge into the greater whole. That is the divine dance and we are all in it.

The beauty is that all this happens by itself. We do not have to do anything to make it happen. Indeed, the more we try to control the process, the more difficult it is for us.

All spiritual awakening is about surrender to what is. We awaken to the beauty of what is already there. Our own deep beauty. The profound beauty of the beloved. The essential perfection of life as it unfolds.

part two

practice

types of practices

Spiritual practice can be pared down to its essential elements. The first is the practice of self acceptance. The greatest obstacle to self acceptance is your self-judgment: the continuous stream of critical thoughts and negative feelings about yourself. As you become aware of these negative thoughts/feelings, you detach from them and move to a deeper level of self-awareness.

The second essential element of spiritual practice is acceptance of others. The greatest obstacle to the acceptance of others is your judgments about them. These judgments of others are really reflections of your own unconscious fears about yourself. You often don't know that you have these fears until you project them onto someone else. That person then shows you the fears that operate within you at an unconscious level. By owning your own fears and not making others responsible for them, you deepen in your acceptance of others.

The third essential element of spiritual practice is acceptance of each situation as it unfolds in your life. The greatest obstacle to your acceptance of what the moment brings is your attachment to the past and your expectation of the future. By surrendering the past and meeting the future without rigid expectations you are able to stay in the flow of your life.

Spiritual practice is cyclic and repetitive by nature. By constantly performing a practice, you learn to master it. Simple moment-to-moment awareness is the highest practice. It is performed whenever you bring your focus totally into the present. To practice, just breathe and give your attention fully to whatever you are doing. Be in your life without liking or disliking it. Just be present, without interpretation or evaluation. If you can do this practice often, other spiritual practices are unnecessary.

Daily practice involves a certain set period of time, such as half an hour or an hour, spent in silent awareness and inner centering. During this time, you focus on your breathing, become aware of your thoughts and feelings and appreciate the perfection of life as it unfolds. This practice can be done alone or with a partner. Daily practice can be augmented by including body-centered meditations such as Hatha Yoga or Tai Chi.

In addition to daily practice, a weekly spiritual ritual helps you integrate your personal practice into the life of the community. Setting aside time each week for communion with God and connection with one's spiritual family is the essence of the Sabbath. The Affinity Group process (described later) provides a simple tool for creating spiritual community in one's life.

Monthly rituals open the core spiritual community to friends and family members. It is celebratory in nature and open to all who are curious to learn more. Through pot luck suppers, devotional singing and other inspirational activities for people of all ages, a safe, loving environment is created in which people learn to deepen their trust in themselves and each other.

Quarterly and yearly rituals connect the group and its extended family with the community at large and with other spiritual communities from different traditions.

The strength of each level of practice depends on the integrity of the level that precedes it. Daily practice is strengthened by moment to moment awareness. Weekly spiritual community is strengthened by daily spiritual rituals performed by individuals. And extended community gatherings are strengthened by affinity group practice.

The ideal of all spiritual practice is to extend one's self acceptance to embrace family and friends, community and humanity at large. In this way, inner peace becomes peace in the world.

daily practice

awareness meditation

Sitting Version: Sit in a comfortable position. Breathe deeply into your belly and be aware of your physical sensations, thoughts and feelings. Just accept whatever your experience is in the moment. Don't try to manipulate your experience or make your judgments or negative feelings go away. Just be aware of whatever is present in your consciousness.

Walking Version: Walk with your eyes open. You can do this in any setting: on a city street or in a forest. Breathe deeply into your belly and be aware of your physical sensations, thoughts and feelings. Just accept whatever your experience is in the moment. Don't try to resist it or embellish it. Just be with it, breathing in a deep, but relaxed way.

Do either of the above exercises for at least ten or fifteen minutes each; if your attention wanders, just bring it gently back. The goal is simply to be present with your experience as it unfolds in a non-judgmental way. As you practice, you will be able to do this awareness exercise for longer periods of time. You will also spontaneously come to it at times when you feel stressed and need to practice.

acceptance meditation

Sit in a comfortable position and breathe deeply into your belly as you did in the exercise above. Be aware of your sensations, your thoughts and your feelings and accept them. Accept them whether you like them or not, just because they are your experience in this moment. Scan through your physical body, your emotional body and your mental body. Get in touch with all that you are experiencing now in this moment. If judgments come up, tell yourself "I see that I am judging so and so." If anger comes up, tell yourself "I see that I am angry at so and so." Be aware of what you are experiencing without judging it. Don't make your experience bad or good. Whatever it is, it is acceptable. Get your arms around it. Just be with what is happening for you in a compassionate way.

The goal in this exercise is not to make judgments and negative feeling states go away, but to bring love to the places in us that feel unloved, wounded or rejected. When you accept your experience exactly as it is without trying to change it, you bring unconditional love to yourself.

After performing this exercise alone, you may want to try it with a partner. Do this practice facing your partner with eyes open or closed, or you may alternate back and forth, first closed, then open. Let your attention be focused on your partner. Be aware of everything that comes up for you when you experience your partner. Again, don't try to make your judgments and negative feelings toward your partner go away; just be aware of them and accept them. By accepting your relationship and all your feelings about it just as it is, without trying to change it, you will be bringing unconditional love and acceptance to the relationship.

You may also do this exercise as a walking meditation. Walk in a place where you are likely to see other people. As you encounter each person, be aware of what you are thinking and feeling and let it be okay. Tell yourself that the person is acceptable as he or she is, regardless of what fears or judgments are coming up for you. Breathe and accept everyone as he or she is. Breathe and accept your judgments. Let everything be as it is and just be present with it. Let your awareness encounter all living things in this way, plants, animals, trees, rocks, and so on. Let your awareness encounter everything in this way: even the sound of traffic, sirens or heavy equipment working on the street. Just be present with everything you encounter and with all of your sensations, feelings and thoughts.

The more you practice this exercise, the more it will happen for you spontaneously when you encounter someone or something that disturbs you and seems to threaten your peace.

listening 1

You can do this exercise with your partner or with any other person with whom you wish to have clear communication. As you begin this practice, please acknowledge to one another that anything communicated in this exercise will be considered confidential and will not be repeated to anyone.

Now you be the listener. Let your partner talk from the heart for five minutes about anything she feels strongly about (the more personal the issue the better). Do not interrupt under any circumstances. Listen deeply and be present for your partner as she talks. As your partner talks, give her your undivided attention. Make eye contact. Keep your heart open.

If your attention drifts, bring it gently back. If you find yourself making judgments about what your partner is saying, become aware of your judgments and bring your attention gently back to what she is saying. If you find that you are agreeing or disagreeing about what your partner is saying, become aware of the fact that this

47

issue has a charge for you and bring your attention back to your partner.

When your partner is finished sharing, tell
her what it felt like to listen without judgment. Ask
her what it felt like to be listened to in this way.
Now give each other a hug and get ready to
switch roles. Take a moment to recenter and
make the transition to the role of speaker. When
you are ready, repeat the exercise with you
speaking and your partner listening to you.

listening 2

Do the first part of the previous exercise.
When your partner is done sharing, repeat back to
him as honestly and non-judgmentally as possible
what you heard him say. Use your partner's language and phraseology as much as possible.
Emphasize the components your partner felt most
strongly about. Now let your partner tell you how
accurate he feels your recounting of the communication was and how deeply he felt listened to.

Then switch and, after you have shared,
allow your partner to repeat back to you what he

heard you say. Then tell your partner how accurate he was and how deeply you felt heard.

weekly practice

affinity groups

An Affinity Group is a gathering of people who want to love and accept each other unconditionally. They know that in attempting to do so, their fears and judgments will come up for healing. They are committed to creating and maintaining a safe, loving space, where they can move through their fears, heal old wounds and take responsibility for their present experience.

If there is someone who has worked with this process, he or she should be asked to facilitate. If not, anyone who feels drawn to facilitate can do so. The facilitation role can also rotate through the group. Ultimately, the group will not need a facilitator, because the members of the group will "own" the guidelines and make sure they are followed.

The following Purpose, Guidelines and Agreements should be read at every meeting of the Affinity Group.

1. Purpose: to give and receive unconditional love, acceptance and support. To create a safe, loving, non-judgmental space in which we can open our hearts and move through our fears.

2. Guidelines
   - Remember our purpose: we are here to love and accept one another, not to judge, analyze, rescue or try to fix one another.
   - We agree to share from our hearts and be honest about what we are thinking and feeling.
   - When our judgments come up about someone, we will be aware of them and gently bring our attention back to the person speaking.
   - We will not interrupt anyone's process. We will give the person sharing our undivided attention. We will not engage in cross talk.
   - We will take 30 seconds in silence to acknowledge each person's sharing.

- We will not monopolize the group's time and attention. We will yield the floor to others in the group who have shared less than we have.

- We will make "I" statements, not "you" statements. We will take responsibility for our own experiences and respect the experience of others. We will not assign "our" meaning to something someone else has said.

- We will not hide our hurt or angry feelings. We will share them honestly, without trying to make others responsible for how we feel.

- If someone shares a hurt or angry feeling with us, we will acknowledge how he or she feels. We will not defend ourselves or try to justify our words or actions. We will share any feelings that come up for us.

- We will stay in the present moment. We will not bring up the past or future, unless they are happening for us here and now.

- We will keep everything that is said in the

group confidential.

- We will honor the silence, knowing that it offers us an opportunity to become more deeply present to ourselves and others.
- If we feel that our group is going "off pur-pose," we will ask for a moment of silence, during which our group can re-center and remember its purpose.
- Remembering that we won't do this process perfectly, we will be gentle with ourselves. We will use whatever transpires in the group as an opportunity to practice forgiveness.

3. Agreements

We commit to:

- Honor the purpose of the group
- Practice the guidelines
- Be on time
- Attend every meeting of the group (if an emergency arises, we will make sure the facilitator knows the situation).

Prospective group members who don't feel comfortable with the purpose, guidelines and agreements of the group should not participate in the group process.

The ideal Affinity Group size is 8-10 people. With that size group, each person has time to share and be heard in a two hour timeframe. Smaller groups are acceptable. Larger groups are discouraged unless the members are already experienced in the Affinity Group Process.

Affinity Groups are designed to meet once per week for approximately two hours. An eight to ten week commitment is suggested. When that commitment is fulfilled, the group can be reconfigured, with some people leaving and new people coming in. However, it is suggested that members give thought to how they can bring the process into other settings in their lives where it might be helpful. In this way, groups do not become ingrown and the process can extend to others who can benefit from it.

Since the prototype Affinity Group exists for the spiritual practice of its members, the content for each group session is simply the thoughts and feelings of its members. Members are asked to share what is most significant and highly charged for them in their life experience, staying in the present as much as possible. The more authentic and honest the sharing is, the deeper people can go in moving through shame and blame and opening to healing.

Any group in which the guidelines are followed is an Affinity Group. Sharing does not have to be thorough or profound. Growth can and does occur for us in staying present for other members of the group, even when their sharing seems guarded or superficial. Above all, the goal must be to keep the space safe and supportive for all members.

Affinity Groups can be topic-oriented, as long as the guidelines are followed. Affinity Groups can focus on topics such as relationships, career, service, and so forth. The content for topic groups is always the personal experiences of members. For example, a group of employees can be asked to share what they value most about their jobs and what they find most frustrating. In this case, the process insures that each person is heard. Differences can then be better understood and respected, and consensus areas can be more easily recognized.

Affinity Groups are a powerful tool for improving communication and morale in hospitals, nursing homes, schools, prisons, community associations, and so forth. They help groups of people accept each other as equals and work together more effectively.

interfaith worship service

The Interfaith Worship Service can be undertaken by itself or as an outgrowth of the Affinity Group process. The goal of the service is to bring people together to share their creative gifts and to participate in community with one another. To help create a safe, loving, non-judgmental space for all members, Affinity Group guidelines are followed.

Participants are encouraged to co-create the worship room and service by offering their decorating skills, artwork, gardening, musical talents and so forth. The Sufi Dances of Universal Peace and simple inclusive music and ceremonies are used to help people connect at the heart level. As much as possible, the atmosphere of the fellowship encourages respect for all spiritual traditions, even though a particular tradition might be emphasized.

Ideally, several Affinity Groups would join together to co-create the Interfaith Worship Service, which would be open to anyone in the community. New people coming in would have the option of joining Affinity Groups as room becomes available. In this way, every fellowship member could experience the depth of love, acceptance, and equal connection found in the Affinity Group, thereby bringing to the larger congregation a depth of personal experience coherent with the group's purpose.

water meditation

Find a stream, a waterfall, or a beach where the surf is breaking. The sound of moving water is profoundly healing, Sit in a comfortable place and listen to the sound of water. Water tells us non-verbally that everything is acceptable as it is. Let the water speak to you. Like the water, your life is moving. All you have to do is move with it. All you have to do is let go of your worries and be present in your life. Like the water, you don't know where you are going or what obstacles will be found in your way. Like the water, you will flow around these obstacles and fulfill your destiny. You don't need to know what your destiny is to fulfill it. You just need to be present in your life.

When you are ready, take a walk along the water's edge, continuing to listen to the sound of water. Now you are moving too. Let life dance inside of you as the water dances in the stream or in the surf. Everything in is flow. Life itself is a flowing forth, an unfolding dance.

mountain meditation

Choose a mountain that you can climb fairly easily. Try to find one that has a view of the surrounding countryside. Climb up the mountain in silence. If you want you can use the Awareness Meditation or the Acceptance Meditation.

When you reach the summit, look at the buildings, the land, the water, the trees that lie below. Notice how different they look from this perspective.

Now close your eyes and see your life from the mountaintop perspective. Notice how certain things that seemed important now seem fairly insignificant. Notice how other things that seemed insignificant now seem important.

As you walk down the mountain, consider how you can take the mountaintop perspective with you, integrating it into your daily life.

service

Volunteer to do something on a weekly basis that helps other people. Choose something that you can do easily without a great deal of planning or deliberation. When it is time to do your service, be one-pointed about it. Focus totally on the work you are doing. Be clear that your purpose is to be helpful. Work with joy, clarity and enthusiasm. Work without expecting anything in return. Be aware of how you feel when you are giving unconditionally. Each time you approach your service, bring a fresh attitude and a renewed willingness to it.

If once a week is too difficult for you, make a monthly commitment to service. Do not do this exercise out of guilt or sacrifice. Do it as a joyful experience of giving unconditionally.

devotional singing and dancing

Invite musicians to join with community members once per week in singing devotional songs and doing devotional dances from different spiritual traditions. Choose songs and dances which are spiritually uplifting, repetitive and easy to learn. The Dances of Universal Peace are particularly inspirational and help to create an open-heart space.

nurturing your partnership

Do something your partner would like you to do with him or her. Vow to see only the positive in this activity, even if it is difficult for you to do so. Make sure that your partner understands that you are doing this activity just once, unless it turns out that you really like it.

Partners can take turns doing this exercise, which helps to develop flexibility and demonstrate caring. Start with things that are relatively easy for each of you to do and, if you have a positive experience, progress from there to more difficult activities.

monthly practice

new moon retreat

The new moon is a time for self-nurturing and self-communion. Find an inspirational place to spend two or three days and arrive at least one day before the old moon disappears. As the old moon wanes, get in touch with that aspect of your emotional experience which needs to be released. Let go of judgments, grievances, disappointments which you are still carrying with you. As you prepare to receive the energy of the new moon, remember that everything that happens in your life can be used in a helpful way. See how the mistakes of the past can help you understand more clearly what you do not want and that, in turn, helps you be clear about what you do want. Be grateful for the relationships in your life that are helping you to learn to honor yourself. Gratitude for the lessons of the past helps insure that you won't repeat those lessons or, if you do, that you will do so more gently.

As the new moon comes in, be clear about what you do want in your emotional life. Get in touch with the positive changes in attitude and behavior which are required of you in order to bring about greater happiness and integrity in your experience. Vow to say no to people or situations that do not honor you and to wait patiently for people and situations which do honor you.

Understand how you have betrayed yourself in the past by saying yes when you wanted to say no. Instead of blaming the person who accepted your invitation, take responsibility for your behavior and realize that you can change it. Your happiness depends on your ability to honor yourself. Take a few minutes and brainstorm some ways that you can do wonderful nurturing things for yourself in the coming month. Visualize yourself saying yes to activities that will help you learn to trust yourself, bond in safe ways with other people and give and receive love and emotional support.

Write these ideas down in your new moon journal, so that you can refer to them on a daily (or at least weekly) basis during this lunar cycle. And return to your life taking increased responsibility for your happiness and well-being, and freeing others from blame for your emotional distress.

If you take time each month to go on retreat at the new moon, you will find that you learn how to take much better care of yourself. You learn how to tune into your emotional body more completely. You see how many of your thoughts, desires, and flights of fancy ignore the needs of your emotional body for regularity and consistency, opening you up to experiences which upset or over-extend you emotionally, depleting your energy and self-confidence. You learn the importance of having a physical and emotional rhythm in your life, which you learn to respect. Once you learn to honor and respect that rhythm, you will find that others give you the space to do so. Monthly retreats will help you learn what you require to feel good emotionally and give you the clarity and strength to stay committed to your emotional health for the rest of the month.

couples retreat

A special version of this retreat can be held for couples who want to focus on their relationship. In this case, each partner would follow the self-communion routine previously described, but additional time would be devoted to understanding what is nurturing and supportive to the emotional health of the relationship. Couples can agree to goals and rituals they can perform during the month which will help them release negative emotions and stay emotionally connected through the inevitable ups and downs of their life together.

It is suggested that each partner attend an individual retreat first and practice taking responsibility for his or her emotional well-being for a while before attending a couples retreat. Couples retreats can and should build on skills learned in the individual retreat process.

community gathering

Once per month — during the full moon, if possible — gather people in your community together for a pot luck dinner, devotional singing, and the Sufi Dances of Universal Peace. People can come from Affinity Groups, Interfaith Services or the community at large. Let everyone – people of all ages and backgrounds – be welcome. This is a simple, easy way for people to feel connected to one another and to experience the emotional support of a loving community. Through this celebratory event, newcomers are introduced to weekly activities in which they might want to participate and the core members of the community are able to reach out to attract the new members which will keep the community dynamic and healthy.

yearly/quarterly practice

vision quest

There comes a time for all of us in which we lose our sense of purpose. Life seems stale or meaningless, or perhaps we feel overwhelmed by all of the pressures in our life. When times like this come, it helps to leave our routine and enter a quest to re-discover the motivating vision of our lives. That vision is ever changing as we grow, achieve our goals, and establish new priorities. Yet there is an aspect of that vision which does not change. It is the essence of who we are and what our life is about.

When we are aware of our essence and able to act on it consistently, we feel energized and sustained. But nobody is able to do this all the time. It is all too easy to become involved in the dramas of other people and forget why we are here. When we forget for a long time, something rises up within us and says "Enough! This won't work any longer." When that moment comes, the vision quest has begun.

When you begin your vision quest, you do not know where you are going. That is the nature of the quest. So don't hang onto a routine that isn't working just because you don't know where to go. Of course you don't know. That's the whole point.

You can do your vision quest in your living room if your living room is a nurturing place away from the stresses and routines of your existence. But most people find it helpful to go to an inspirational place. Wherever you go, choose a place that will feed your soul and allow plenty of time for silent reflection.

Understand that your journey is a spiritual one and that everything that happens to you on your quest is significant. Even if you don't understand the meaning of chance events and encounters right away, you will have insights later. So be open and receptive. Take risks. Invite possibilities. Trust your hunches and intuition. Explore. Have Fun. Don't plan any more than you absolutely have to. Allow plenty of room for spontaneity.

Walk through the open doors even though you don't know where they lead. Stay away from the closed doors even though you think there's something behind them you want or you need.

Be in the flow of your life without expectations. If you let go, you will be guided downstream. If you resist and swim upstream, you will find yourself very frustrated, but that is perhaps what you most need to learn: that you can't control your life at the ego level. Until your ego loosens its hold on your life, you might get your feet wet, but the rest of your body won't experience the river. To know the river and be guided by its current, you must stop trying to control what happens to you.

A vision quest should last for at least a week, but a month or even a year might be appropriate. You'll know how long you need. When you do self-communion rituals on an ongoing basis, taking a week to ten days once a year is usually fine. But when you have been lost in the same routine for twenty years, you might need a full year for your vision quest. Some people call this a sabbatical.

But that suggests you are coming back to the same routine. When you go on a vision quest, you have no idea what you are coming back to. You just know you have to leave.

When you return from your quest, you will have a strong intuition about what your life purpose is and how you can begin to honor it in the moment. Don't worry if you know only what step one is. That is all most people know. The other steps will reveal themselves as you learn to trust your guidance and begin to walk the path of your heart.

seasonal gatherings

Four times per year the seasons change. Each season has its own special meaning. Spring is a time for sowing, summer a time for flowering, fall a time for harvesting, and winter a time for resting and renewal.

As participants in the natural cycle, we can harmonize and learn from the seasons as they change. Each season lasts for 91 days beginning approximately 45 days before the equinox or solstice and ending 45 days after it. Spring begins after the first week in February and ends after the first week in May. Summer begins after the first week in May and ends after the first week in August. Autumn begins after the first week in August and ends after the first week in November. Winter begins after the first week in November and ends after the first week in February.

During the spring season, we can crystallize our vision, build support for it and lay the groundwork for its implementation. During the summer season, we can actively implement our vision and share it with the maximum number of people. During the autumn season, we can enjoy the fruits of our labor, get feedback on what worked and what did not work, and begin to revise our strategies for next year. During the winter season, we can feel gratitude for our successes, come to terms emotionally with our failures, let go of what did not work, listen for new ideas and nurture them quietly in our hearts.

Spiritual gatherings can be planned to reflect the meaning of these seasonal cycles.

Winter conferences and retreats should be times of grieving and letting go of the past, inner listening and visioning for the future. Spring gatherings should be times when we come together with other people, discover where our visions are in harmony and where we can network with and/or support each other. Summer events should be times when we promote our ideas and products, learn from the creative expressions of others, and generally share and celebrate who we are and what we do. Autumn events should be times when we recognize the good that we have done, come to terms with our mistakes, and help each other see where improvements can be made in the future.

While it is not helpful to use this understanding of the solar cycle in a rigid way, using it flexibly can help us align our human energies with the energies of the sun that sustain life on our planet.

other quarterly cycles

A similar quarterly cycle occurs every day of the year with midnight corresponding to the winter phase, dawn corresponding to the spring phase, noon corresponding to the summer phase, and sunset corresponding to the autumn phase. Since most of us sleep at night and work during the day, we tend to be aligned reasonably well with the daily cycle.

Another quarterly cycle occurs with the phases of the moon. In the lunar cycle, the new moon corresponds to the winter phase, the first quarter moon corresponds to the spring phase, the full moon corresponds to the summer phase, and the three quarter moon corresponds to the autumn phase. We are far less attuned to the lunar cycle now that the majority of us do not farm or work the land for our livelihoods. As a result, we are emotionally disconnected from nature in ways that do not serve us or the planet we live on. Tuning in to the lunar cycle on a regular basis can be very healing for us and for the environment in which we live.

part three

learning to
listen

the greatest joy

There is at all times and in all situations a course of action that honors all of the people involved, but it cannot be found until the thoughts and feelings of all people have been heard.

When people are heard, they feel honored and respected. They can extend caring and courtesy to others who have different points of view. And so a variety of viewpoints and perspectives can be considered. The best decisions are made when this happens.

When each person has input into a decision-making process, she helps to shape the action that is taken and therefore owns the process. She is included in the process, without excluding others.

When the ideas of people are not heard and they are not included in the decision-making process, they feel that no one cares about them. When children or adults feel cut off and uncared for, they react in hurt or angry ways. Any action that is taken on their behalf will be resented, if not opposed.

All any one wants is to be heard, to be cared about and respected. These are universal human concerns. As a husband or wife, we should extend this caring and respect to our partner. As a parent, we should extend it to our children. As a community, we should extend it to all of our members: rich or poor, black or white, able-bodied or disabled.

Thomas Jefferson argued that each of us has certain inalienable rights. Yet, as a practical matter, some of us are not willing to grant to others the most basic of all rights: the right to have a voice in the decisions that affect them. But even when we agree that others should have a voice, it doesn't mean that we are willing to listen. And, unless we are willing to listen, what does having a voice mean? What does free speech mean if we are always putting our hands over our ears?

Our society says that everyone has a right to speak, but it cannot make us listen. It cannot insure that we will hear what others say to us or that they will hear what we say to them. Hearing has always been optional. It has always been a matter of choice.

Hearing others is a form of loving them. And love has never been successfully legislated. You cannot make somebody love another person, nor can you make somebody listen to another.

Many of us believe that we listen, but it's not true. Listening, if we did it deeply and fully, would totally transform our lives.

To find out how well you listen, try a little experiment. For the next half hour, pay attention to everything your ears can hear: the sound of the wind or rain, the hum of your computer or refrigerator, the person who calls on the telephone, the voice of your wife when she is reminding you about dinner with your inlaws. Just listen without judgment. And if judgments come up, remember that you aren't listening: you're judging.

Don't respond in any way except to acknowledge that you have heard. If you are responding, you have stopped listening.

Just listen. Try it for a half hour. Then do a full hour. Then listen for a whole morning or afternoon. You will be amazed how little you actually hear most of the time.

We think that we hear one another, but we don't listen very long or very deeply to each other. We are easily distracted by our own thoughts or by events happening in our environment.

When we really "hear," we feel acceptance, compassion, love, respect. We don't want to give the other person a lecture or try to fix him or her. We just feel good that the person felt safe enough to communicate honestly with us.

When we really "hear" another person, we hear ourselves. We know it could be us talking. There is that equality. There is that rapport.

Hearing is a shared experience. It is an experience of communion.

Let us be honest. We are not in communion with one another most of the time. We are not listening deeply to each other. We are not fully present.

Knowing that, we can choose to be present. We can choose to listen. We can take our hands away from our ears and look each other in the eyes. We can "hear" with our heart and not just with our ears. We can offer each other love and respect.

Listening to other people is a great blessing that we offer them. It is not a casual or insignificant act, but an act of great purpose and beauty, an act that will inspire and uplift. That is how Jesus listened, not just with his ears, but with his heart, with his whole being.

So when we listen to others, let us listen not to agree or to disagree, but simply to hear what their experience is. And when we speak to others, let us speak not to obtain attention or approval, but to communicate what is in our hearts and minds.

Our greatest joy is not to find agreement with others, but to experience hearing and being heard deeply and without judgment. This can be achieved in every encounter.

attention and intention

In order to listen deeply, we must pay attention to what the other person is saying. We can't be preoccupied with our own thoughts and feelings. We can't be tired and cranky. Paying attention to another person requires energy and clarity. It requires patience and respect for what the other person wants to communicate to us. As long as we respect the intention of the person speaking, it is easier to pay attention to what he or she is saying.

But if the person speaking attacks us and we take offense, we lose our attention instantly. We lose our attention because we stop respecting the person's intention. We think the person wants to hurt us. And we turn off, or we react and attack back. As soon as we take offense, as soon as we see another's intention as anything less than honorable, we stop being able to listen. Communication ceases. Communion is broken.

To listen requires not only attention, but awareness of our intention toward the other person. If we are feeling attacked, then we don't want to hear the other person. We want to attack back or defend ourselves. When this happens, we must be aware of it and acknowledge what is happening. To try to listen when we are feeling attacked is foolish. There is no way that we can do it. Better to bring the issue up directly and say "I would really like to hear what you are saying, but I can feel myself turning off. Can we both take a moment to check out where we are coming from and if we really want to be doing this now?"

Better to call "time out" then to engage in attack and defense. Better to come back when we are not tired, or cranky, or defensive, than to try to listen when we are. Listening takes energy and attention. It takes receptivity to and compassion for the other person. When these qualities are not present in our consciousness, we should not be trying to listen. Nor should we be trying to speak to another person.

Communication doesn't just happen by itself. It requires the right intention and attention. With these present, communication not only works, it is a sacred experience. Without these qualities, communication is impossible, and words are said that will have to be atoned for later.

give peace a chance

You would not go to a fancy dance dressed in greasy clothes. Don't come to a meeting with someone you care about tired, cranky or suspicious of their motives. Nothing good can come of this.

Prepare for your meeting by being alert, receptive to the other person and clear about your own intentions. Come able to feel the other's good intention and able to pay attention to what he or she has to say. This sets the stage for a sensitive, respectful exchange.

Before you eat a nice meal, you set the table. Before you speak to someone you care about, you check your energy level and your state of consciousness. If you bring anger or resentment to the table, you are likely to leave the table with them reinforced.

You don't sit down at the table to eat when you are already full. Don't come to the table of communion full of negative thoughts and feelings. If you do, your intention will not be worthy.

If you go to the negotiating table ready to attack, how can you come away having made peace? If you want to make peace, come in peace. Speak peacefully. Listen peacefully. Then, even if you disagree, understanding is still possible.

Ask yourself always: "what do I want here? Do I want peace or do I want war? Do I want to be right or do I want to be happy? Do I want a solution that honors both of us, or do I want my way to prevail?" And please be honest with yourself.

If you say you want peace when in fact you are angry and resentful, you only hurt your chances for reconciliation. Better to recognize your anger and resentment and back off. Better to take time to be with your anger and resentment until you feel them shift. When the shift occurs and the softness returns to your heart, then you can return to the table. Then you will come wanting peace, and then you will be giving peace a chance.

the dance of energy

More often than not, when two people approach each other weak or needy, wanting attention or approval, both will be disappointed. That is because neither person is in a position to give. To give, one must be feeling good about oneself. Then that goodness naturally extends to the other person.

If one person is feeling good and the other person needs a little attention or cheering up, a productive exchange is possible. In this case, the stronger person helps to energize the weaker one, who is then able to respond on an equal basis. Equality is the key here. As long as both people play the role of giver and receiver, the dance continues to rejuvenate. But if one person is always doing the giving and the other the receiving, the energy slows down and we have a dance of statues. Rigid patterns of relating do not bring about the kind of energetic renewal needed in a partnership.

When there is equality between two people,

there is a balance of giving and receiving in the relationship. Neither person feels that he or she is doing most of the giving or receiving. While we understand that this equality is important in our relationships, we don't always know how it originates.

To be equal with another, we must be as willing as the other person is to take responsibility for loving ourselves. If we are more willing or less willing than our partner is, we will outgrow the relationship or our partner will. Relationships prosper only when there is an initial equality and both people grow together in responsibility.

Contrary to popular opinion, the relationship does not exist to "fill the person up" to the brim so that he no longer needs to take responsibility for loving himself. Rather, the relationship exists to reflect back to him all those times when he feels needy and looks to the other person to fill him up. If he can become conscious of the fact that he feels disappointed or betrayed because the other person isn't meeting his needs, and if he can learn to love and nurture himself in those moments, he can use the relationship to wake up.

Of course, he won't always do this, nor will his partner. There will be times when he expects his partner to make him happy and she expects him to meet her needs for love. And in those moments, there will be anger, hurt, disappointment, and betrayal, all of which will require forgiveness if the two people are to return to self-caring, self-responsibility, and healthy patterns of relating. We mustn't underestimate the tremendous significance of ongoing forgiveness practice in a relationship. Without it, anger becomes resentment and hurt becomes hypersensitivity to the words and actions of the other. Battle lines are drawn in the sand and crossed unconsciously in countless instances of mutual trespass and betrayal. In the process, old childhood wounds are reopened and trust is seriously damaged, if not completely destroyed.

Without forgiveness, there is no way out of the downward spiral of mutual projection and blame. Without forgiveness, mistakes are cast in stone. No one softens or forgets the pain of the past. Like a heavy anchor, the weight of each mistake is carried forward into the future. If you want an image of hell, this one isn't a bad one.

But forgiveness brings us over and over again from hell to heaven, from anger and blame to understanding and responsibility. Forgiveness cancels the debt. It wipes the slate clean so that we can begin again.

Every couple must start their relationship over again countless times. They must embrace the mistakes they have made and begin to learn from them.

Couples who want their relationship to be free of mistakes are setting impossible standards. They will never be able to achieve outward perfection, as individuals or as partners. There will always be arguments, separation, fears and resentments. A good relationship is not one in which mistakes are not made, but one in which mistakes open the door to learning, growth, adjustment and reconciliation.

We must judge our progress not only based on how many times we have betrayed each other, but also based on how many times we have made amends. If we insist on counting our mistakes, we must also count our moments of forgiveness. A relationship is not just an invitation to judgment and despair, but also an invitation to tolerance and illumination.

Every relationship we have asks us to learn to love and accept ourselves unconditionally. It seems to ask us to love and accept the other without conditions. But that is just the mask, the appearance. The face behind the mask does not belong to our partner, but to ourselves.

When we learn how to feed ourselves, feeding our partner is not difficult. When we learn how to love and nurture ourselves, appreciating and supporting our partner are not arduous tasks. The love we learn to give to ourselves is automatically offered to everyone who comes into our energy field. But try to give that love to someone else when we have not given it first to ourselves and the gift is questionable indeed.

When we enter a relationship, we are not excused from the ongoing process of learning to love and accept ourselves in each moment. On the contrary, we are given the same course with a more difficult curriculum. Now, we are not only responsible for loving ourselves when we feel sad or lethargic, but loving ourselves when we feel de-energized and depressed and our partner does too. If we didn't learn the undergraduate curriculum, we can't expect to do well in graduate school.

This doesn't mean that we have to be enlightened to have any hope of realizing happiness in our relationships. It means that we have to give up the romantic myth that being with a partner is somehow "easier" or "more wonderful" than being alone. It isn't! Or if it is easier, it is also harder. And if it is more wonderful, then it is also more harrowing.

When we give up the romantic illusion, we can accept the "harder" with the "easier," the pain with the joy, the darkness with the light. Relationships are vessels for learning. They intensify our journey in every way. They make it more poignant, more heartwrenching, more ecstatic.

But the lesson of relationship is the same lesson we are learning in our journey alone. It is the lesson of forgiving ourselves when we make mistakes, loving ourselves when we feel unlovable, and giving ourselves energy and attention when we feel physically or emotionally drained. It is not about finding someone else to do this for us. Nor is it about doing it for our partner when he or she is needy. It is about doing it for ourselves when we are needy. And doing it for ourselves when our partner is needy.

And then if we have done it for ourselves, we will have something left to offer our partner. If we have learned to dance with our own shadow, we can dance with our partner, or with our partner's shadow, without tripping over our own toes.

Whatever the dance we appear to be doing — no matter how tricky the footwork — we can be sure that our essential responsibility never shifts from self to other. When the other asks us to dance, the dance with self speeds up. When other arrives, responsibility to self deepens.

self and other

We have so much confusion about what is self and what is other. The word "other" itself is confusing. What is an other? Is an other not a self? Maybe it is not our self, but is it not some-body's self? And how is somebody's self different from our self?

The truth is that there is no difference. Each self is the same.

Personality is different, but self, core being, is the same. As self, we are absolutely equal. As personality, we are not equal, nor are we the same.

When I see you as other, I address the dif-ferences, the inequalities I perceive between us. When I see you as self, I address the commonal-ities I perceive between us.

As self, you are my equal and the language I use to address you is the language of love, respect, acceptance, gratitude. That language endears me to you and you are likely to address me in a similar way.

As other, you are better or worse than me. You are skinnier or fatter, richer or poorer, more or less intelligent. As other, you are not my equal. And the language I use to address you is laced with judgment, be it positive or negative. That language may flatter you or criticize you. You may like it or dislike it. But it does not endear me to you, and you are likely to respond to me with your own judgments.

All communication begins with intent. And intent is demonstrated in the address. If I address you as self, I seek equality and communion. If I address you as other, I see some form of inequality and disconnection.

What is my intent? How do I address you: as self or as other? As an equal or not as an equal? As a friend, or as an enemy?

It doesn't matter what I say so much as how I say it. What is my tone of voice? Is it harsh and judgmental or soft and accepting? What is my state of consciousness? Am I calm or agitated? What is the energy and intention behind my words? If I know that, I know everything I need to know. I know if I am blessing or attacking. And so do you.

You know when I speak to you as other, not as self. And you know that at these times there is very little likelihood that we are going to have a satisfying conversation. So you get out of the way as quickly as possible. You sidestep the energy and go for a walk. Or, if you must, you let me know that you don't feel good about the way the conversation is going and you'd prefer to have it at another time when we both feel more connected to each other.

You ask to be addressed as self, not as other. And you do that by addressing me as self. You do that by being kind to me even when I am not being kind to you. You are firm and clear, but gentle and loving. You know self is there in me and you call out to that. You don't address me as other, just because I address you that way.

When you address me as self, you stay in yourself. You stay in your truth and your strength. You keep who you are. When you address me as other, you lose yourself. You leave your essence, your strength, your integrity.

As you address me, so do you become. Address me as other and you become other. You betray yourself. Address me as self, and you become self. You honor who you really are.

You can never be who you really are and treat me badly. When you are treating me badly, you are giving yourself away. You are investing in the false self, the ego, the illusion. You are pretending to be someone else. I can respond to you by pretending, by putting on my mask, or I can stay as I am. If I stay as I am, I respond to you with acceptance and love. I am gentle and kind to you, even when you are not being nice to me. By being who I really am, I connect with who you really are, and I invite both of us to give up our fear-based masks.

Are you self or are you other? That is the question I must ask myself in every moment that we share together. The answer to that question also tells me where I am. It tells me if I am in my true self or my false self.

When I see you as other, I become an other to myself. I become split within. My integrity is compromised. When I see you as self, I heal the split within myself and regain my own integrity. How I see you and how I see myself are intricately related.

Is there such a thing as self and other? No, there is only self, or there is only other. The two do not exist together. When self is present, there are no others. When others are present, there is no self.

The choice is a simple one and an absolute one. It is a choice born in every moment we spend together.

self is ecstatic

When self is present, there is nothing that is not self. Self is indivisible. It is essentially whole and coherent.

Only when we leave self behind do we experience separation, division, competition, incoherence. But "leaving self behind" is an illusion. If you are in the self, how can you leave

97

self? Of course you can't. You can only pretend to leave. And in that pretense is the experience of "other."

If we could not experiment in this way — pretending to leave the source — how would we know who and what we are? Only by pretending to be something other than self, can self know what it is.

Other is, then, an invention of consciousness.

In reality, there is no other. There is just self.

In reality, there is no separation, only oneness.

In reality, there is no pain, only ecstasy. But to know ecstasy means to know pain. To know oneness means to know separation. To know self means to know other. That is what the journey of consciousness is all about.

But when the journey is over, you go home. When you know that other is just self in disguise, you don't see other anymore. When you don't see other anymore, you stop giving yourself away. You stop leaving home.

You awaken. You know who you are. External events and circumstances may not change, but your relationship to them changes substantially. Now, there is nothing in your experience that is not part of you. Everyone who comes and goes is self. Everything that happens is the play of self.

the ecstatic moment

In the ecstatic moment, there is no wrong-making, no finding fault, no self-righteousness. In the ecstatic moment, everything is acceptable as it is. People are acceptable as they are. There is no need to fix anyone or anything. Criticism is absent. Consciousness of lack does not exist. Problems are not perceived.

Ecstasy is possible right now or in any other moment of time. But it cannot be experienced when you are finding fault with another person or with yourself. Ecstasy cannot be experienced when you have the perception that something is wrong, that something needs to be improved, fixed, or changed. Ecstasy happens only when your judgments of self and other dissolve. It happens only when you get down to your essence, which is at peace, which is in acceptance of all that life brings.

The only obstacle to an ecstatic life lies in your own mind. How you think, how you perceive things, determines whether you are happy or sad, fulfilled or dissatisfied. Ecstasy, happiness, peace are not dependent on anything in the external world. They are dependent only on the content of your consciousness at any given time. If you can stop seeing lack, if you can stop finding fault, if you can stop trying to fix, you will connect with the ecstatic life energy which is moving through you.

If you think you have been unfairly treated, you won't be feeling ecstatic. If you are holding on to old grievances, you won't be feeling energized and whole. Even if you believe that you were treated unfairly, you could think about it in a way that would make you feel good about yourself. And when you feel good about yourself, you don't hold onto grievances.

But let's be clear: feeling good about yourself is a full time job. Not holding grievances, not seeing lack, not trying to fix someone else or yourself — this is a moment-to-moment practice. It takes all of your time and attention. As soon as you stop paying attention and wander into feeling sorry for yourself, the moment ceases to be ecstatic.

That is why all of the great spiritual teachers have asked us to "wake up" and "pay attention." They have asked us to look at our own thoughts and the feelings associated with them so that we can see how they impact our experience. They have asked us to tune into our own creative experience, which is by nature subjective.

In our minds and hearts we create the world. With our thoughts and feelings we determine our experience. If we are positive about life, it is because we are thinking certain thoughts and feeling certain feelings. If we are negative about life, it is because we are thinking other thoughts and having other feelings. There is nothing eso-teric about this. It is quite mechanical.

But since we aren't always aware of what we are thinking and feeling, sometimes we forget that we are generating our own experience. Then we begin to believe that something is happening to us from the outside. And we try to change that outside event or circumstance, believing that it is the cause of our unhappiness. But, of course, that is nonsense. The cause of our happiness lies in the thoughts we are thinking and the feelings we are having. And, frankly, we do not know what they are.

So the first act of spiritual practice is simply "awareness." Tune into thoughts and feelings. Observe. Witness. Get to know the content of consciousness: our fears, assumptions/beliefs, and emotional reactions. The first act is to turn our attention away from the world to our own subjective experience.

That doesn't mean that our attention won't ever come back, that we will become a zombie meditating in a cave in the Himalayas. Our attention can move back outward once we have fully witnessed our own subjective experience. Once we know how we create happiness or suffering in our own heart/mind, then we can be helpful in the world. We can help others see where meaningful change originates. But we can't do that as long as we are living our lives in reaction to the thoughts and feelings of others. We can't help others until we learn to help ourselves.

Awareness is the first step. And it is the last step. There may be other steps in between or there may not. There may be actions taken spontaneously in the moment. Or there may be refraining from actions in the moment that would lead to suffering and attachment. But we always return to awareness, because that is where the ecstasy is.

Simple awareness of what we are thinking and feeling in any moment. That is all. No judgment about what we are thinking and feeling. No trying to fix. Just simple awareness of thought and feeling, rising and falling like waves on the beach. The observer looking at himself. Accepting himself as he is. Heart open, eyes alert. Breathing in deeply, breathing out deeply. The ecstatic moment. It is always there.

May you find it when you need it. Just

remember: everything is okay just the way it is. Every thought you have has already been for-given. Just keep breathing. Just keep blessing yourself. Just keep bringing love and acceptance. The rest will take care of itself.

part four

an

angel's

song of

waking

rainbow crib

If joy is available right now, why do we put off experiencing it? Why do we postpone feeling the ecstasy that is available to us? What is more important? Is there a bigger priority?

When we feel joy, our whole life lights up. When we feel joy, our light extends to everyone in our experience. In our presence, people who hide in the darkness of judgment and criticism suddenly see the light that shines inside themselves.

Joy is God's work. It is the active ingredient in a love that embraces all things.

If you want to do God's work, find the light that lies in your mind and heart. Feel the heat that comes into the heart center when you breathe and bless your experience. Feel the fire in the heart that comes from your gratitude, your appreciation of your life just the way it is. Feel the warmth and the love that extend from your heart when you accept the people in your life just the way they are.

All this is can be experienced, here and now.

You are the light of the world, but you do not know it. You do not know it because you have not looked deeply enough into your own heart.

Take a moment to look. Take a moment to see who you really are.

Do not take your cues from the world anymore. Take your cues from the light that dances in your heart. Then your eyes will sparkle when others lose hope.

Then, when skies are dark in the east, you will point to the light that comes flooding through the dark clouds in the western sky. And, when people turn around, they'll see something new and exciting in the eastern sky: a column of many colored light arching up through the blue black clouds. Sudden and luminous.

Because you see the light in yourself, light comes to the world. Because you feel joy in this moment, the warmth in your heart is given wings. There is no one who is not touched by your love, your caring, your attention.

Sitting at home, breathing, the whole world

awash with light. Deep purple and violet and red penetrating the black clouds, hands of light reaching from one end of the horizon to the other. A rainbow. A simple song of joy from one person's heart to another.

Take the time now.

The rainbow will not be here tomorrow, or even in fifteen minutes. The beauty in this world will go unnoticed if it is not embraced right now. Nothing is more important than opening your eyes and opening your heart right now.

Let us take a deep breath and begin. The crib is awash with light and someone is singing. We can hear it now. Don't you hear it?

> "Hushabye, don't you cry.
> It's time to wake up, little baby.
> It's time to wake up
> and see the rainbow ponies,
> running in the rain:
> green leaves turning
> to orange and yellow.

Autumn has come
on the wind and rain
and we are letting go
of our sadness.
Letting go, little one
like the leaves on the tree
and the rainbow colors
in the window.

Wake up, little one.
It's time to get up and see
all the pretty ponies.
They have been here before
but you were sleeping.
Don't sleep any more.
There's a rainbow
knocking on the door
and a dance of leaves
fluttering in the window.

Don't sleep anymore,
There's an angel knocking
on your door,

with a rainbow bird
and a singing snake
calling you to wake.
And the sun's going down
on the west side of town
so there's not much time.
to wake up, little one,
so wake up, wake up
wake up.

earning our wings

Waking up means learning to pay attention to what is. It means becoming emotionally present, and mentally alert. It means not getting lost in the mind — not spacing out or obsessing — nor getting lost in the heart — not being reactive or numbing out. It means being centered, rooted, balanced, yet flexible, like a tree swaying in the breeze.

It means weathering the ups and downs of life with poise and dignity. Celebrating the new leaves and the singing of the sap, the explosion of color as they reach maturity and surrender, whole or broken, to the push and pull of the wind. Everything in life has its seasons. The mind and the heart are no exception.

We cannot stop the seasons from turning. We cannot stop ourselves from growing older, from coming face to face with our own death, the final surrender. With all respect to Dylan Thomas, let us not "rage against the dying of the light," but let us go gently, like a leaf fluttering in the wind, trusting the ground that has nurtured it from root to branch to wing. Having anchored ourselves in the ground of being, all of our blossoming — however unruly or magnificent — can return to that ground without suspicion or distrust. Resting in God in this moment, why would we not rest there in our last breath? Trusting our life, why would we not trust our death.

It is only when we don't show up for life that death is terrifying. It's time for all of us to begin to show up. To begin seeing the stunning beauty that surrounds us. To start building the trust in ourselves and others that brings the gift into all its glory. And enables us to surrender it completely, trusting not only what has been given to us, but what we have given. Letting it go do its work, knowing that it is not perfect, but that it is the best we could do. And knowing that is enough. That will always be enough.

God does not ask us to be perfect. She does not ask us to be mistake free. She asks only that we learn to receive the love that is there for us and find a way to pass it on to others. She wants us to receive so that we may have something to give, and to give so that we may be able to receive again more deeply. She wants us to come full circle. She wants us to keep exercising the muscles of our heart.

Some things take time. Learning to give and receive may take time. But it may also happen spontaneously. No matter how much time is taken, the moment of breakthrough is the same. Where trust was absent, it becomes present. From the trembling of the leaf at the branch's end, comes the dance of letting go. The dance of trusting self and other.

There's nothing wrong with taking time.

There's nothing wrong with getting ready. But if we spend all our time getting ready, we won't learn to trust. We won't learn that we can take risks successfully, that we can act in good faith without knowing the outcome.

In every honest act of giving or receiving, there is trust. There is risk. There is the feeling that one is not ready and may never be ready. But that feeling must not hold us back. We can waver and tremble before we reach out to give or receive the gift. But in the end we must do it. We must trust, even when we are scared, even when we think we might fail. We must do it, because that is what each one of us has come to do.

Just as the tree has come to grow leaves and surrender them, we have come to embrace our gift and offer it unconditionally to the world. That is our purpose. It is a simple one.

We need to keep it that simple.

Let our timing be what it will. Let us prepare as long as we must. But let us also remember that the moment for giving and receiving is now. If we don't do it now, in this moment, it may not be done.

Sometimes a great being — a divine messenger — comes along. And he says: "It's okay. You can do it." He helps us get through our fear. And whatever the result, he says "Great. That's exactly what was needed. We can work with that."

When we have such an angel in our lives, we are grateful indeed. But sometimes we wait for such a messenger and he never arrives. We want someone to tell us it will be okay, that our gift will be acceptable the way it is. But, in the silence and the discomfort of waiting, we learn to tell that truth to ourselves. And if this happens, we have been given an even greater gift.

If you have a guardian angel, congratulations. And if you don't, may you know that you have been doubly blessed. For what has not been given to you, you must become.

Better to earn your wings than to depend on someone else's.

It is a lonely journey learning to give yourself the love that you seek from others. But once you know how to do it, that love can never be taken away from you. It's a gift that will be constantly given and received.

That is God's greatest gift to you. Won't you claim it?

You thought you were going to a school that would teach you whom to love and when. But the class you were assigned had a different curriculum. You got the angel class. The master curriculum. The one that gave you the only gift that could not be taken away from you. The gift of eternal life and love.

Once you have learned to love yourself in all your unruliness and complexity, with all your contradictions, your ambivalence, your self-deceptions, once you have learned to love the dark side, the hidden lunar surface of your consciousness — the anger and sadness, the self-judgment and feelings of powerlessness — you have mastered the hardest part of the curriculum. The rest of your lessons here will be easy ones. Practicing what you know. Passing the gift on to others. Loving them when they attack you. Telling them "you can do it" when they are trembling in fear and lack of self-confidence. Reminding them that whatever happens is acceptable. It can be worked with.

In other words, you begin your angel apprenticeship. Right here on earth, in this body. Isn't that a trip? Now when people ask for divine intervention, YOU get to appear in their lives. No, not Jimmy Stewart's celestial friend. You. The angel in training.

Remember? You are the light of the world.

And now you know it.

Congratulations.

You have earned your wings!

P aul Ferrini is the author of numerous books which help us heal the emotional body and embrace a spirituality grounded in the real challenges of daily life. Paul's work is heart-centered and experiential, empowering us to move through our fear and shame and share who we are authentically with others. Paul Ferrini founded and edited Miracles Magazine, a publication devoted to telling Miracle Stories offering hope and inspiration to all of us. Paul's conferences, retreats and Affinity Group Process have helped thousands of people deepen their practice of forgiveness and open their hearts to the Divine presence in themselves and others. For more information on Paul's workshops and retreats or The Affinity Group Process, contact Heartways Press, P.O. Box 181, South Deerfield, MA 01373 or call 413-665-0555.

New Titles from Heartways Press
by Paul Ferrini

The Relationship Book You've Been Waiting For!

**The Seven Spiritual Laws
of Relationship: A Guide
to Growth and Happiness
for Couples on the Path**
144 pages paperback $10.95
ISBN 1-879159-39-2

"The most important books I have read. I make them like a bible." Elizabeth Kubler-Ross, M.D.

the seven
spiritual
laws of
relationship

A Guide to Growth and Happiness
for Couples on the Path

Paul Ferrini
Author of the bestselling book Love Without Conditions

This simple but profound guide
to growth and happiness for couples
will help you and your partner:

- Make a realistic commitment to one another
- Develop a shared experience that nurtures your relationship
- Give each other the space to grow and express yourselves as individuals
- Communicate by listening without judgment and telling the truth in a non-blaming way
- Understand how you mirror each other
- Stop blaming your partner and take responsibility for your thoughts, feelings and actions
- Practice forgiveness together on an ongoing basis

These seven spiritual principles will help you weather the ups and downs of your relationship so that you and your partner can grow together and deepen the intimacy between you. The book also includes a special section on living alone and preparing to be in relationship and a section on separating with love when a relationship needs to change form or come to completion.

Our Surrender Invites Grace

Grace Unfolding: The Art of Living A Surrendered Life
96 pages paperback $9.95
ISBN 1-879159-37-6

As we surrender to the truth of our being, we learn to relinquish the need to control our lives, figure things out, or predict the future. We begin to let go of our judgments and interpretations and accept life the way it is. When we can be fully present with whatever life brings, we are guided to take the next step on our journey. That is the way that grace unfolds in our lives.

Part IV of the Reflections of the Christ Mind Series is Hot off the Press

Return to the Garden
Reflections of The Christ Mind, Part IV
$12.95, Paperback
ISBN # 1-879159-35-X

"In the Garden, all our needs were provided for. We knew no struggle or hardship. We were God's beloved. But happiness was not enough for us. We wanted the freedom to live our own lives. To evolve, we had to learn to become love-givers, not just love-receivers.

We all know what happened then. We were cast out of the Garden and for the first time in our lives we felt shame, jealousy, anger, lack.

We experienced highs and lows, joy and sorrow. Our lives became difficult. We had to work hard to survive. We had to make mistakes and learn from them.

Initially, we tried to blame others for our mistakes. But that did not make our lives any easier. It just deepened our pain and misery. We had to learn to face our fears, instead of projecting them onto each other.

Returning to the Garden, we are different than we were when we left hellbent on expressing our creativity at any cost. We return humble and sensitive to the needs of all. We return not just as created, but as co-creator, not just as son of man, but also as son of God."

Learn the Spiritual Practice
Associated with the Christ Mind Teachings

Living in the Heart
The Affinity Process
and the Path of
Unconditional Love
and Acceptance
Paperback $10.95
ISBN 1-879159-36-8

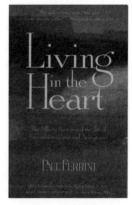

The long awaited, definitive book on the Affinity Process is finally here. For years, the Affinity Process has been refined by participants so that it could be easily understood and experienced. Now, you can learn how to hold a safe, loving, non-judgmental space for yourself and others which will enable you to open your heart and move through your fears. The Affinity Process will help you learn to take responsibility for your fears and judgments so that you won't project them onto others. It will help you learn to listen deeply and without judgment to others. And it will teach you how to tell your truth clearly without blaming others for your experience.

Part One contains an in-depth description of the principles on which the Affinity Process is based. Part Two contains a detailed discussion of the Affinity Group Guidelines. And Part Three contains a manual for people who wish to facilitate an Affinity Group in their community.

If you are a serious student of the Christ Mind Teachings, this book is essential for you. It will enable you to begin a spiritual practice which will transform your life and the lives of others. It will also offer you a way of extending the teachings of love and forgiveness throughout your community.

Now Finally our Bestselling Title on Audio Tape

Love Without Conditions, Reflections of the Christ Mind, Part I
by Paul Ferrini

The Book on Tape
Read by the Author
2 Cassettes,
Approximately 3.25 hours
ISBN 1-879159-24-4 $19.95

Now on audio tape: the incredible book from Jesus calling us to awaken to our own Christhood. Listen to this gentle, profound book while driving in your car or before going to sleep at night. Elisabeth Kubler-Ross calls this "the most important book I have read. I study it like a Bible." Find out for yourself how this amazing book has helped thousands of people understand the radical teachings of the master and begin to integrate these teachings into their lives.

Heartways Press

"Integrating Spirituality into Daily Life"
More Books by Paul Ferrini

With its heartfelt combination of sensuality
and spirituality, Paul Ferrini's poetry has been
compared to the poetry of Rumi.

• **Crossing The Water:**
  Poems About Healing and
  Forgiveness in Our Relationships

The time for healing and reconciliation has
come, Ferrini writes. Our relationships help us
heal childhood wounds, walk through our
deepest fears, and cross over the water of
our emotional pain. Just as the rocks in the
river are pounded and caressed to rounded
stone, the rough edges of our personalities are worn smooth in the
context of a committed relationship. If we can keep our hearts open,
we can heal together, experience genuine equality, and discover what
it means to give and receive love without conditions.

With its heartfelt combination of sensuality and spirituality, Paul
Ferrini's poetry has been compared to the poetry of Rumi. These
luminous poems demonstrate why Paul Ferrini is first a poet, a lover
and a mystic. Come to this feast of the beloved with an open heart
and open ears. 96 pp. paper ISBN 1-879159-25-2 $9.95.

"The most important book I have read. I study it as I have a Bible."
— Elisabeth Kübler-Ross, M.D.

Miracle of Love

Reflections of the Christ Mind · Part 3

Paul Ferrini

"Paul Ferrini is a modern-day Kahlil Gibran — poet, mystic, visionary, teller of truth."
— Larry Dossey, M.D.

• Miracle of Love: Reflections of the Christ Mind, Part III

Many people say that this latest volume of the Christ Mind series is the best yet. Jesus tells us: "I was born to a simple woman in a barn. She was no more a virgin than your mother was." Moreover, he tells us, the virgin birth is not the only myth surrounding his life and teaching. So are the concepts of vicarious atonement and physical resurrection.

Relentlessly, the master tears down the rigid dogma and hierarchical teachings that obscure his simple message of love and forgiveness. He encourages us to take him down from the pedestal and the cross and see him as an equal brother who found the way out of suffering by opening his heart totally. We too can open our hearts and find peace and happiness. "The power of love will make miracles in your life as wonderful as any attributed to me," he tells us. "Your birth into this embodiment is no less holy than mine. The love that you extend to others is no less important than the love I extend to you." 192 pp. paper ISBN 1-879159-23-6 $12.95.

• Waking Up Together: Illuminations on the Road to Nowhere

There comes a time for all of us when the outer destinations no longer satisfy and we finally understand that the love and happiness we seek cannot be found outside of us. It must be found in our own hearts, on the other side of our pain. "The Road to Nowhere is the path through your heart. It is not a journey of escape. It is a journey through your pain to end the pain of separation."

This book makes it clear that we can no longer rely on outer teachers or teachings to find our spiritual identity. Nor can we find who we are in relationships where boundaries are blurred and one person makes decisions for another. If we want to be authentic, we can't allow anyone else to be an authority for us, nor can we allow ourselves to be an authority for another person.

Authentic relationships happen between equal partners who take responsibility for their own consciousness and experience. When their buttons are pushed, they are willing to look at the obstacles they have erected to the experience of love and acceptance. As they understand and surrender the false ideas and emotional reactions that create separation, genuine intimacy becomes possible, and the sacred dimension of the relationship is born. 216 pp. paper ISBN 1-879159-17-1 $14.95

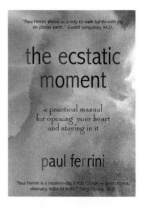

• The Ecstatic Moment:
A Practical Manual for Opening
Your Heart and Staying in It

A simple, power-packed guide that helps us take appropriate responsibility for our experience and establish healthy boundaries with others. Part II contains many helpful exercises and meditations that teach us to stay centered, clear and open in heart and mind. The Affinity Group Process and other group practices help us learn important listening and communication skills that can transform our troubled relationships. Once you have read this book, you will keep it in your briefcase or on your bedside table, referring to it often. You will not find a more practical, down to earth guide to contemporary spirituality. You will want to order copies for all your friends. 136 pp. paper ISBN 1-879159-18-X $10.95

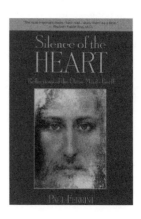

• The Silence of the Heart:
Reflections of the Christ Mind,
Part II

A powerful sequel to Love Without Conditions. John Bradshaw says: "with deep insight and sparkling clarity, this book demonstrates that the roots of all abuse are to be found in our own self-betrayal. Paul Ferrini leads us skillfully and courageously beyond shame, blame, and attachment to our wounds into the depths of self-forgiveness...a must read for all people who are ready to take responsibility for their own healing." 218 pp. paper. ISBN 1-879159-16-3 $14.95

126

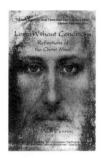

• Love Without Conditions: Reflections of the Christ Mind, Part I

An incredible book from Jesus calling us to awaken to our Christhood. Rarely has any book conveyed the teachings of the master in such a simple but profound manner. This book will help you to bring your understanding from the head to the heart so that you can live the teachings of love and forgiveness. 192 pp. paper ISBN 1-879159-15-5 $12.00

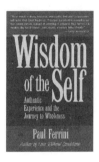

• The Wisdom of the Self

An exploration of authentic experience and the journey to wholeness. "Your life is your spiritual path. Don't be quick to abandon it for promises of bigger and better experiences. You are getting exactly the experiences you need to grow. If life seems too slow or uneventful for you, it is because you have not fully embraced the situations and relationships at hand...To know the Self is to allow everything, to embrace the totality of who we are, all that we think and feel, all of our fear, all of our love." 229 pp. paper ISBN 1-879159-14-7 $12.00

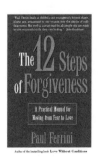

• The Twelve Steps of Forgiveness

A practical manual for healing ourselves and our relationships. This book gives us a step-by-step process for moving through our fears, projections, judgments, and guilt so that we can take responsibility for creating the life we want. With great gentleness, we learn to embrace our lessons and to find equality with others. A must read for all in recovery and others seeking spiritual wholeness. 128 pp. paper ISBN 1-879159-10-4 $10.00

• The Wounded Child's Journey Into Love's Embrace

This book explores a healing process in which we confront our deep-seated guilt and fear, bringing love and forgiveness to the wounded child within. By surrendering our judgments of self and others, we overcome feelings of separation and dismantle co-dependent patterns that restrict our self-expression and ability to give and receive love. 225pp. paper ISBN 1-879159-06-6 $12.00

• The Bridge to Reality

A Heart-Centered Approach to *A Course in Miracles* and the Process of Inner Healing. Sharing his experiences of spiritual awakening, Paul emphasizes self-acceptance and forgiveness as cornerstones of spiritual practice. Presented with beautiful photos, this book conveys the essence of *The Course* as it is lived in daily life. 192 pp. paper ISBN 1-879159-03-1 $12.00

• From Ego to Self

108 illustrated affirmations designed to offer you a new way of viewing conflict situations so that you can overcome negative thinking and bring more energy, faith and optimism into your life. 144 pp. paper ISBN 1-879159-01-5 $10.00

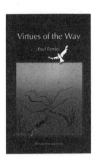

• Virtues of The Way

A lyrical work of contemporary scripture reminiscent of the Tao Te Ching. Beautifully illustrated, this inspirational book will help you cultivate the spiritual values required to fulfill your creative purpose and live in harmony with others. 64 pp. paper ISBN 1-879159-02-3 $7.50

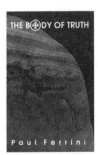

• The Body of Truth

A crystal clear introduction to the universal teachings of love and forgiveness. This book traces all forms of suffering to negative attitudes and false beliefs, which we have the ability to transform. 64 pp. paper ISBN 1-879159-02-3 $7.50

• Available Light

Inspirational, passionate poems dealing with the work of inner integration, love and relationships, death and re-birth, loss and abundance, life purpose and the reality of spiritual vision. 128 pp. paper ISBN 1-879159-05-8 $12.00

Poetry and Guided Meditation Tapes
by Paul Ferrini

The Poetry of the Soul

With its heartfelt combination of sensuality and spirituality, Paul Ferrini's poetry has been compared to the poetry of Rumi. These luminous poems bring us face-to-face with the Beloved. With Suzi Kesler on piano. $10.00 ISBN 1-879159-26-0

The Circle of Healing

The meditation and healing tape that many of you have been seeking. This gentle meditation opens the heart to love's presence and extends that love to all the beings in your experience. A powerful tape with inspirational piano accompaniment by Michael Gray. ISBN 1-879159-08-2 $10.00

Healing the Wounded Child

A potent healing tape that accesses old feelings of pain, fragmentation, self-judgment and separation and brings them into the light of conscious awareness and acceptance. Side two includes a hauntingly beautiful "inner child" reading from *The Bridge to Reality* with piano accompaniment by Michael Gray. ISBN 1-879159-11-2 $10.00

Forgiveness: Returning to the Original Blessing

A self healing tape that helps us accept and learn from the mistakes we have made in the past. By letting go of our judgments and ending our ego-based search for perfection, we can bring our darkness to the light, dissolving anger, guilt, and shame. Piano accompaniment by Michael Gray. ISBN 1-879159-12-0 $10.00